IN THE BEGINNING
A CHILD'S BEGINNER BOOK OF BIBLICAL HEBREW

SAWYER D. MORANVILLE

www.ingramcontent.com/pod-product-compliance
Lightning Source LLC
Chambersburg PA
CBRC091205010526
44107CB00021B/1252

Sawyer D. Moranville, *In the Beginning: A Child's Beginner Book of Biblical Hebrew*

CC0 2023 by Sawyer D. Moranville

This work is freely given. All of this publication may be shared, translated, sold, or copied freely without limitation and without permission. To learn more about this open license, visit https://copy.church/free/

Design: Sawyer D. Moranville
Artwork: AI image generator accessed through Canva.com

For the free PDF please visit *LinguaDeoGloria.com*

Lingua Deo Gloria Publishing
ISBN 979-8-218-33118-4

General Notes

Every Hebrew word that is listed in this book appears in the Hebrew Bible with the exception of the word "colors" (צְבָעִים) and a few words in the dedication to my daughter, which were drawn from modern Hebrew because of their absence in the Hebrew Bible. For the most part, I attempted to stay away from the use of modern Hebrew words, because my main goal is that this book will serve students of the Hebrew Bible. The Hebrew words listed appear in both the singular and plural forms (the only exceptions are words that appear only in singular or plural forms in the Hebrew Bible).

The colors in Hebrew were challenging to present because colors are dependent upon concrete objects in the Hebrew Bible and are not often seen as abstract colors as we may see them today. Further, the color תְּכֵלֶת was a challenge to represent. Many say that the color is a form of violet, while more modern evidence suggests that it may have been a sky blue. I went with the latter, though I am open to correction on this matter for any potential future edition.

Concerning the precious stones, many translations differ on which Hebrew word represents which gemstone. I primarily used the Legacy Standard Bible's (LSB) translation of Exodus 28:17-20 as the basis for deciding these matters.

Regarding the animals in the pictures, I am not fully aware how some of the animals would have looked during Bible times. For instance, how can we know what kind of cows were present in ancient Israel over three thousand years ago? Some suggest from bone evidence that they were a type of Zebu cow that originally migrated from India. Since this is a children's book, I will not go further into this complex discussion. I chose a form of the Zebu cow as the model for the cows that appear in this book. Once again, I am open to correction on this point.

None of the categories that I presented in this book contain comprehensive lists. For instance, there are many more unclean and clean animals in the Hebrew Bible. I often chose those animals which were most common (although, there are exceptions). The same goes for the geographical features, the parts of the body, types of food, etc.

It seems like the ancient Israel calendar was not divided into four main seasons but two. Perhaps this was dependent upon the important seasonal activities of planting and harvesting.

Finally, all of the images presented in this book were produced by an AI image generator through the book production application that I use. However, all other technical details and formatting work was done by my hand.

Acknowledgements

Thanks to Andrew and Bethany Case who corrected errors in this book, gave helpful feedback, and provided access to necessary technological resources for the production of this book. Thanks to my good friend, Ben Eisenberg, who helped make this book better by providing spelling feedback. Also, thanks to my grandmother Sally for reviewing the English portions of this book and providing feedback on grammar and spelling. Thanks to my wife who always had good ideas about the structure and organization of this book. Also, for her labors of taking care of our children while I was working on this time-consuming project.

רַבּוֹת בָּנוֹת עָשׂוּ חָיִל וְאַתְּ עָלִית עַל־כֻּלָּנָה (Proverbs 31:29)

Soli Deo Gloria

Introduction

This book is the product of combining two of my great loves in life: my family and the Hebrew Bible. My two-year old daughter has recently been pulling books off the shelf at home and asking her mommy and me to go through them with her. Our household language is English, and therefore she generally pulls English books off the shelf. This has been a joy. Sometimes, however, she pulls a modern Hebrew picture book off the shelf and wants to look through it with us. As time progressed, I realized that there seems to be a vacuum of Biblical Hebrew picture books that we can buy for her to use at home. Because of this, I began to imagine creating a book that would help her learn Biblical Hebrew. I also wanted her to be exposed to the rich beauty of the Word of God and the revelation of the glory of God as we see it presented in the Hebrew Bible. As I was producing other works related to the biblical languages (such as my Hebrew work on Jonah or my Greek work on 1 John), I began to realize that there is a huge need for easy Biblical Hebrew books. Most modern Biblical Hebrew instruction is filled with challenging concepts that my two-year old daughter could never learn. However, she learns very well by looking at pictures. It finally occurred to me that I should produce a Biblical Hebrew picture book for children (and adults!) that would be a delight to the eyes and aid reading comprehension.

My hope and prayer is that this book strengthens love for family, allowing parents who are studying Biblical Hebrew for hours on end to spend less time in their stale offices or dusty library cubicals and more time reading with their children on the couch at home. That is the main reason why I wanted to create this book. I do not want to be in my office all day. I want to be with my daughter and son as they grow up. They have only a few years with us before they mature and move away. Thus, I wanted to create fun ways for my work to intersect with my family. This is the best idea that I had. I hope and pray that this helps you do the same.

הַסֵּפֶר הַזֶּה מֻקְדָּשׁ לְבִתִּי Mercy Waive בְּיוֹם הֻלַּדְתָּהּ הַשֵּׁנִי

תְּפִלָּתִי לַיהוה
תֶּאֱהֲבִי אֶת־אֲדֹנָי בֹּרֵא הַשָּׁמַיִם וְהָאָרֶץ וְיֵשׁוּעַ בְּנוֹ וּמְשִׁיחוֹ בְּכָל לְבָבֵךְ לְעוֹלָם וָעֶד

אֲנִי אוֹהֵב אוֹתָךְ

Table of Contents

חַיּוֹת טְמֵאוֹת 1

חַיּוֹת טְהוֹרוֹת 5

בָּשָׂר 8

צְבָעִים 11

הַשָּׁמַיִם וְהָאָרֶץ 13

אוֹתוֹת וּמוֹעֲדִים 17

מַאֲכָל 20

מִלְחָמָה 23

אֲבָנִים יְקָרוֹת 25

עִיר וּבַיִת 28

מִסְפָּרִים 31

Glossary 37

חַיּוֹת טְמֵאוֹת

 נְמָלָה - נְמָלִים	 דְּבוֹרָה - דְּבֹרִים
 עַקְרָב - עַקְרַבִּים	 לְטָאָה
 נָחָשׁ - נְחָשִׁים	 צְפַרְדֵּעַ - צְפַרְדְּעִים

 כֶּלֶב - כְּלָבִים	 אַרְנֶבֶת
 אַרְיֵה	 זְאֵב - זְאֵבִים
 גָּמָל - גְּמַלִּים	 סוּס - סוּסִים

שׁוּעָל - שׁוּעָלִים

דֹּב - דֻּבִּים

חֲזִיר

חֲמוֹר - חֲמֹרִים

נֶשֶׁר - נְשָׁרִים

נֵץ

חַיּוֹת טְהוֹרוֹת

דָּג - דָּגִים

בָּקָר

אַיָּל - אַיָּלִים

עֵז - עִזִּים

צְבִי - צְבָיִם

צֹאן

יוֹנָה - יוֹנִים

צִפּוֹר - צִפֳּרִים

חָגָב - חֲגָבִים

כֶּבֶשׂ - כְּבָשִׂים

פָּרָה - פָּרוֹת

פַּר - פָּרִים

 אַף - אַפַּיִם	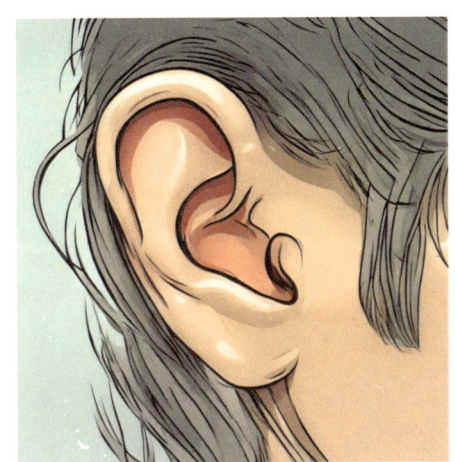 אֹזֶן - אָזְנַיִם
 פֶּה - פִּיוֹת	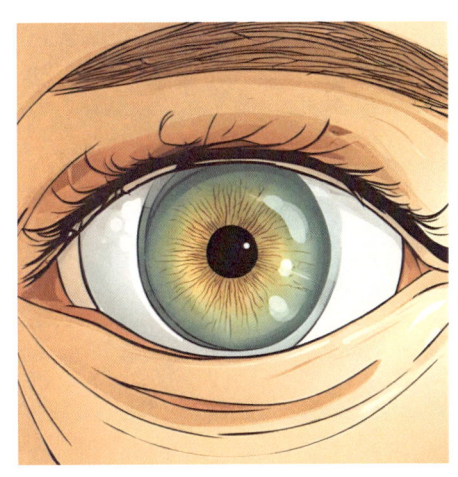 עַיִן - עֵינַיִם
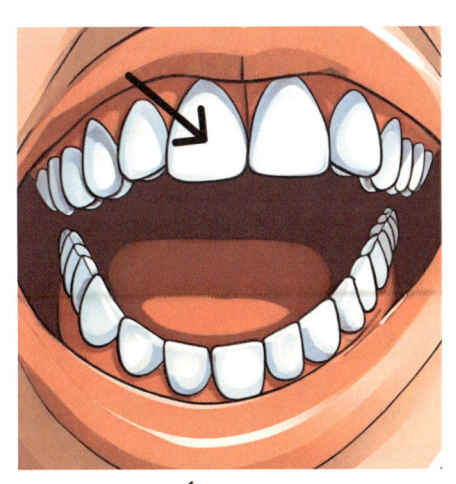 שֵׁן - שִׁנַּיִם	 שָׂפָה - שְׂפָתַיִם

 זָקָן	 שֵׂעָר
 פָּנִים	 רֹאשׁ - רָאשִׁים
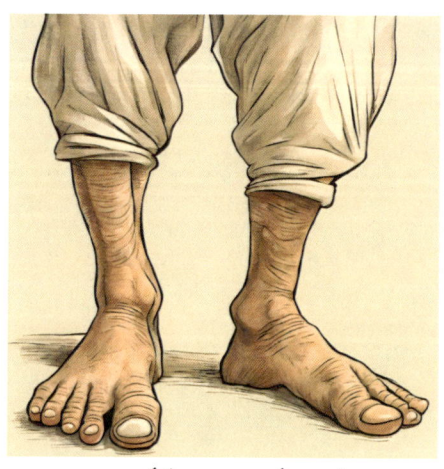 רֶגֶל - רַגְלַיִם	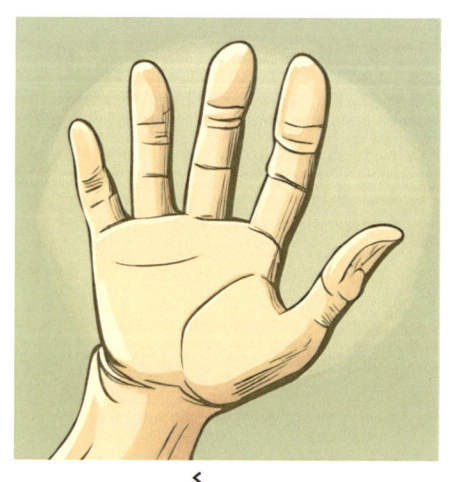 יָד - יָדַיִם

 הָאָרֶץ	 הַשָּׁמַיִם
 יַעַר - יְעָרִים	 נָהָר - נְהָרִים
 יָם - יַמִּים	 מִדְבָּר

נַחַל - נְחָלִים

גִּבְעָה - גְּבָעוֹת

עֵמֶק - עֲמָקִים

אִי - אִיִּים

שָׂדֶה - שָׂדוֹת

הַר - הָרִים

הַשֶּׁמֶשׁ ⇄ הַיָּרֵחַ

בֹּקֶר ‏ עֶרֶב ‏ כּוֹכָב - כּוֹכָבִים

יוֹם - יָמִים ⇄ לַיְלָה - לֵילוֹת

בָּשָׂר - בְּשָׂרִים

לֶחֶם

רִמּוֹן - רִמּוֹנִים

עֵנָב - עֲנָבִים

תְּאֵנָה - תְּאֵנִים

תַּפּוּחַ - תַּפּוּחִים

 קֶמַח	 זַיִת - זֵיתִים
 חִטָּה - חִטִּים	 תָּמָר - תְּמָרִים
 מַיִם	 יַיִן

חֲנִית - חֲנִיתִים

חֶרֶב - חֲרָבוֹת

קֶשֶׁת - קְשָׁתוֹת

חֵץ - חִצִּים

מָגֵן - מָגֵנִים

כּוֹבַע - כּוֹבָעִים

אֹדֶם

סַפִּיר - סַפִּירִים

אַחְלָמָה

בָּרֶקֶת

שֹׁהַם

פִּטְדָה

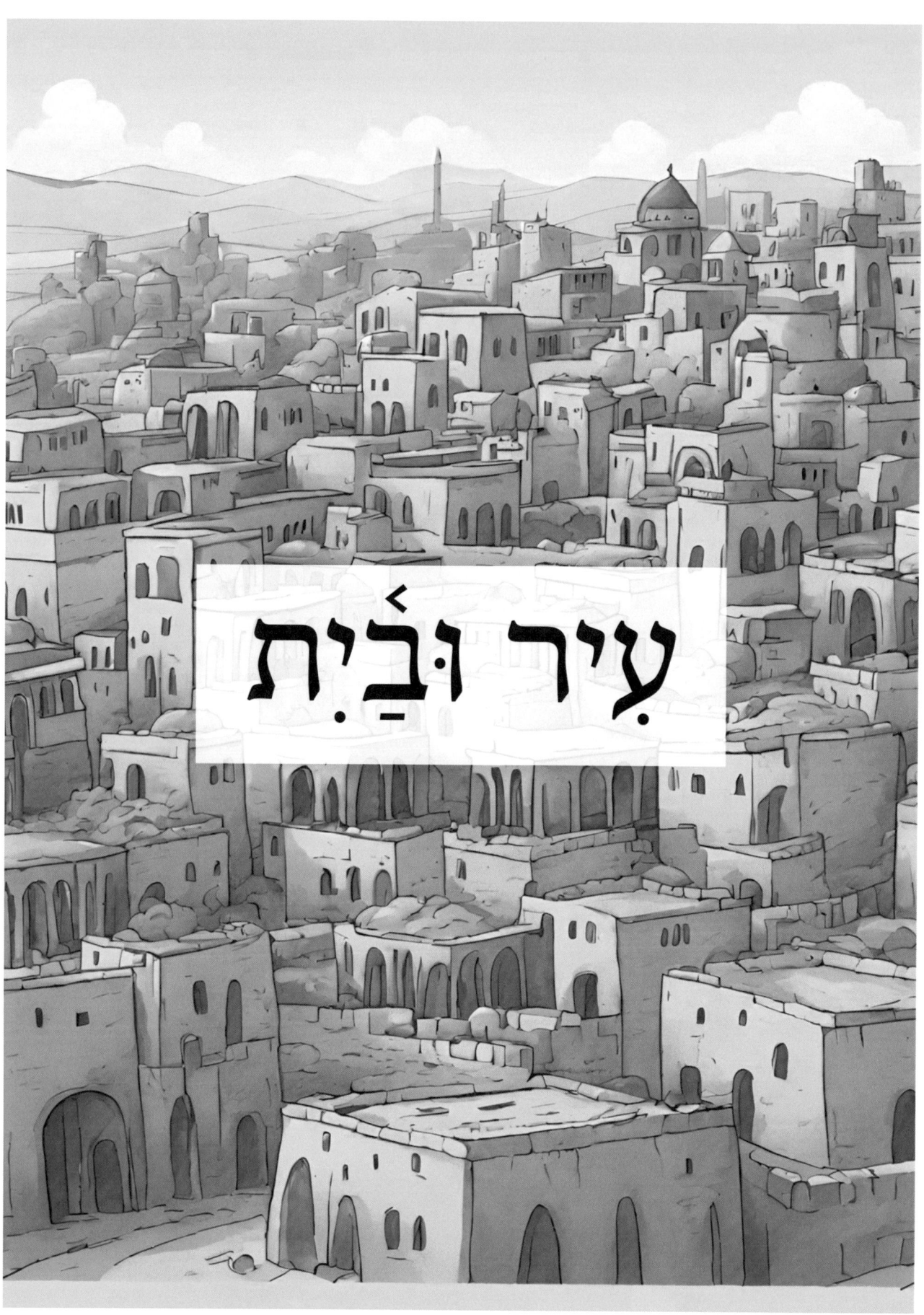

 מִגְדָּל - מִגְדָּלִים	 בַּיִת - בָּתִּים
 בְּאֵר - בְּאֵרֹת	 אֹהֶל - אֹהָלִים
 עִיר - עָרִים	 אַרְמוֹן - אַרְמְנוֹת

כִּסֵא - כִּסְאוֹת

מִטָה - מִטּוֹת

בֶּגֶד - בְּגָדִים

שֻׁלְחָן - שֻׁלְחָנוֹת

סֵפֶר - סְפָרִים

נַעַל - נַעֲלַיִם

מִסְפָּרִים

נְקֵבָה

אַחַת - 1

שְׁתַּיִם - 2

שָׁלֹשׁ - 3

אַרְבַּע - 4

חָמֵשׁ - 5

שֵׁשׁ - 6

שֶׁבַע - 7

שְׁמֹנֶה - 8

תֵּשַׁע - 9

עֶשֶׂר - 10

זָכָר

אֶחָד - 1

שְׁנַיִם - 2

שְׁלֹשָׁה - 3

אַרְבָּעָה - 4

חֲמִשָׁה - 5

שִׁשָׁה - 6

שִׁבְעָה - 7

שְׁמֹנָה - 8

תִּשְׁעָה - 9

עֲשָׂרָה - 10

Glossary

Page 1
חַיּוֹת טְמֵאוֹת - unclean animals

Page 2
נְמָלָה - ant
דְּבֹרָה - bee
עַקְרָב - scorpion
לְטָאָה - lizard
נָחָשׁ - snake
צְפַרְדֵּעַ - frog

Page 3
כֶּלֶב - dog
אַרְנֶבֶת - hare
אַרְיֵה - lion
זְאֵב - wolf
גָּמָל - camel
סוּס - horse

Page 4
שׁוּעָל - fox
דֹּב - bear
חֲזִיר - pig
חֲמוֹר - donkey
נֶשֶׁר - vulture
נֵץ - hawk

Page 5
חַיּוֹת טְהוֹרוֹת - clean animals

Page 6
בָּקָר - cattle, herd
דָּג - fish
עֵז - female goat
אַיָּל - hart, stag, deer
צֹאן - flock (sheep or goats)
צְבִי - gazelle

Page 7
יוֹנָה - dove
צִפּוֹר - bird
חָגָב - locust/grasshopper
כֶּבֶשׂ - sheep
פָּרָה - cow (female)
פַּר - young bull/steer

Page 8
בָּשָׂר - flesh/body

Page 9
אַף - nose/nostrils
אֹזֶן - ear
פֶּה - mouth
עַיִן - eye
שֵׁן - teeth
שָׂפָה - lip

Page 10
זָקָן - beard
שֵׂעָר - hair
פָּנִים - face
רֹאשׁ - head
רֶגֶל - foot
יָד - hand

Page 11
צְבָעִים - colors

Page 12
יָרֹק - green
אַרְגָּמָן - purple
שָׁחֹר - black
לָבָן - white
תְּכֵלֶת - sky blue
אָדֹם - red

Page 13
הַשָּׁמַיִם וְהָאָרֶץ - the heavens and the earth

Page 14
הָאָרֶץ - the earth
הַשָּׁמַיִם - the heavens, the skies
יַעַר - forest
נָהָר - river
יָם - ocean/sea
מִדְבָּר - desert/wilderness

Page 15
גִּבְעָה - hill
נַחַל - wadi
אִי - island/coastland
עֵמֶק - valley
הַר - mountain
שָׂדֶה - field

Glossary Continued

Page 16
cloud - עָנָן
snow - שֶׁלֶג
rain - גֶּשֶׁם
bow (rainbow) - קֶשֶׁת
fire - אֵשׁ
smoke - עָשָׁן

Page 17
signs and seasons - אֹתוֹת וּמוֹעֲדִים

Page 18
harvest-time, autumn - חֹרֶף
summer - קַיִץ

Page 19
the moon - הַיָּרֵחַ
the sun - הַשֶּׁמֶשׁ
star - כּוֹכָב
evening - עֶרֶב
morning - בֹּקֶר
night - לַיְלָה
day - יוֹם

Page 20
food - מַאֲכָל

Page 21
meat/flesh - בָּשָׂר
bread - לֶחֶם
pomegranate - רִמּוֹן
grape - עֵנָב

Page 21 Cont.
fig - תְּאֵנָה
apple - תַּפּוּחַ

Page 22
flour - קֶמַח
olive - זַיִת
wheat - חִטָּה
date fruit - תָּמָר
water - מַיִם
wine - יַיִן

Page 23
war/battle - מִלְחָמָה

Page 24
spear - חֲנִית
sword - חֶרֶב
bow (weapon) - קֶשֶׁת
arrow - חֵץ
shield - מָגֵן
helmet - כּוֹבַע

Page 25
precious stones - אֲבָנִים יְקָרוֹת

Page 26
carnelion - אֹדֶם
sapphire - סַפִּיר
amythest - אַחְלָמָה
emerald - בָּרֶקֶת
onyx - שֹׁהַם

Page 26 Cont.
topaz - פִּטְדָה

Page 27
rock - אֶבֶן
pearls - פְּנִינִים
copper/bronze - נְחֹשֶׁת
iron - בַּרְזֶל
gold - זָהָב
silver - כֶּסֶף

Page 28
city and house/home - עִיר וּבַיִת

Page 29
tower - מִגְדָּל
house/home - בַּיִת
a well - בְּאֵר
tent - אֹהֶל
city - עִיר
citadel/castle/palace - אַרְמוֹן

Page 30
seat of honor/throne - כִּסֵּא
couch/bed - מִטָּה
garment/clothing - בֶּגֶד
table - שֻׁלְחָן
scroll/book - סֵפֶר
sandal/shoe - נַעַל

Glossary Continued

Page 31

מִסְפָּרִים - numbers

Page 32

נְקֵבָה - female/feminine word gender

Page 34

זָכָר - male/masculine word gender

Free Biblical Hebrew and Greek Resources

Lingua Deo Gloria exists to serve the people of God by producing free Biblical Hebrew and Greek products. These comprehensible input tools assist pastors and laymen in their study of the Scriptures. All of our works, including this book, are available for free PDF download at our website LinguaDeoGloria.com.

1 John: A Visual Reader is the first Koine Greek project in the Lingua Deo Gloria Greek Readers series. This work is aimed at helping students grasp the Koine Greek text of 1 John by the service of visual aids and margin notes. The goal is to make the Biblical text understandable to all desiring to read the Word of God in the original Greek!

Jonah: A Visual Reader, is the first Hebrew project in the Lingua Deo Gloria series. It serves Biblical Hebrew students by presenting "Comprehensible Input" (i.e. the use of intuitive pictures and margin notes to help serve readers). Students will feel more comfortable with the Hebrew language and enjoy reading the text without difficult translation.

Ruth: A Visual Reader, is the second project in the Lingua Deo Gloria Hebrew series. This work is aimed at helping students grasp the Biblical Hebrew text of Ruth by the service of visual aids and margin notes. The goal is to make the Biblical text understandable to all desiring to read the Word of God in the original Hebrew!

Philemon: A Visual Reader, is the first Koine Greek project in the Lingua Deo Gloria series to include English glosses for difficult words. Like the Jonah Project, this work is aimed at helping students grasp the Koine Greek text of Philemon by the service of visual aids and margin notes. The goal is to make the Biblical text understandable to all desiring to read the Word of God in the original Greek!

Free Live Hebrew Instruction

Another one of our ministries is teaching spoken Biblical Hebrew online for free. We also do not charge any money for this. Until we raise enough support, spots are limited. However, you may apply to take our 12-week live Hebrew courses through our website. If you would like to see more slots open in the future for yourself or other Christians, we would encourage you to donate.

Support and Connect

If you enjoy this book and find it to be helpful for you and others in learning Hebrew, we encourage you to financially support our work through Patreon. We release all of our products for free PDF download on our website (LinguaDeoGloria.com) and sell our printed books for no profit to keep prices as low as possible for Christians across the globe who want to learn the Word of God in their original languages. These free works take a substantive amount of time to complete. So we would be ever thankful if you decided to financially support this ministry. This will forever remain a free service to the Church of the Lord Jesus Christ.

If you desire to be up to date with materials that we are working on or find out about recently released projects, you may subscribe on our website to receive periodic email updates. These will not be spam emails. You will learn about everything that we are releasing for free to the public.

Errors and Corrections

If you find any errors in this book, please contact us directly at our email address. We are happy to receive your feedback and make this book better for the global Church. Your partnership with us in these matters is valuable!

About the Author

Sawyer Moranville was raised in Montana. He began to study Koine Greek, Classical Hebrew, and Classical Latin at Southern Seminary in Louisville, Kentucky which led to a Master's of Divinity. After graduating, he moved to Jerusalem with his wife to study more Hebrew (where their first child was born). He received a Master's in Classical Hebrew through the Institute for Biblical Languages and Translation (now, The Whole Word Institute). He is pursuing a ThM in Old Testament at Westminster Theological Seminary (WTS) and working for Graterford Bible Fellowship Church outside of Philadelphia.